Original title:
Golden Sands, Blue Waters

Copyright © 2025 Creative Arts Management OÜ
All rights reserved.

Author: Theodore Sinclair
ISBN HARDBACK: 978-1-80581-485-6
ISBN PAPERBACK: 978-1-80581-012-4
ISBN EBOOK: 978-1-80581-485-6

A Symphony of Light and Aqua

Sunshine dances on the shore,
Seagulls squawk, demanding more.
A beach ball flies, a splat! Oh dear!
Who knew a splash would bring such cheer?

Buckets fill with treasures bright,
Crabs perform a comical flight.
With sandy feet and giggles wide,
We try to run, but then we slide!

Merging of Blue and Honeyed Light

A blanket spread beneath the sun,
Ice cream drips, oh what fun!
We chase shadows, skip and prance,
Every drop, a silly dance!

Waves whisper secrets to the shore,
We ride them in, then call for more.
A jellyfish floats by with glee,
Is that a ghost? Or just me?

Nature's Palette at Water's Edge

Flip-flops squeak in rhythmic tune,
Sandcastles rise beneath the moon.
A crab in a hat? What a sight!
Who knew the beach could be so bright?

Paddleboards wobble, laughter rings,
Seashells showcase what joy brings.
With every splash, a grin appears,
Look out! Watch out for those wild cheers!

Radiance on the Water's Canvas

Sun hats bobbing like balloons,
Children sing their silly tunes.
A frisbee flies, a dive, a flop,
And then, oh no! It takes a drop!

Sand crabs plotting great escape,
With every step, a funny shape.
Dolphins smile, we wave back too,
They know just how to make us woo!

Sunlit Embrace

The sun's so bright, it seems to tease,
I squint my eyes and shout with ease,
"Hey, sun, do you think you're bold?"
A tan so dark, I feel like gold!

With flip-flops flapping, I do a dance,
I trip and fall, it's no mere chance,
The sand sticks tight, like it's my friend,
I guess I'll stick around till the end!

Ocean's Gentle Caress

The waves crash in, they pull me near,
I squeal with joy, perhaps some fear,
I dodge a splash, or so I thought,
  Now my hair's a salty knot!

With every wave, I feel the glee,
But watch out, here comes double me!
I laugh so hard, I lose my snack,
  But that sea gull's got my back!

Mirage of Tranquility

I spot a drink, a fancy cup,
I sprint on over, then trip and sup,
The drink spills out, oh what a mess,
I guess it's just my luck, I guess!

The hammock sways, I take a seat,
I dream of lunch, something to eat,
But here comes wind, and off I fly,
I'm just a leaf, and the breeze my guy!

Serenity in the Surf

The seagull squawks, it's quite a chatter,
I toss my crumbs, oh, what's the matter?
A troop of birds descend like ninjas,
My lunch is gone, oh, what's the clinch here?

I build a castle, tall and proud,
Then a wave comes in, oh wow, wow, wow!
My castle, like dreams, goes with a splat,
But hey, I still got my silly hat!

Waves Beneath the Sky

The ocean grins as seagulls squawk,
With flip-flops lost, it's quite the shock.
Sandcastles crumble with a giggly shout,
Who knew a wave could turn you out?

The crabs wear hats, quite a sight to see,
Dancing in circles, as happy as can be.
Don't trip on the towel, it's quite a disaster,
When you're sprinting to flee from a tidal master!

A Promise in Every Tide

The tide rolls in, bringing a surprise,
A rubber ducky with googly eyes!
It's floating past like a little boat,
Beware of the splash from the swimmer's promote!

The beach ball sails and bops on the head,
Of a sunbather snoozing, dreaming in bed.
The sun laughs bright, and sunscreen's a mess,
Who needs to tan, when you can look like a pest?

Moonlit Reflections

At night the waves shimmer, like sequins and beads,
While beachgoers stumble on hidden sea weeds.
"Watch your step!" they holler with glee,
As they slip and tumble into the sea!

The moon hangs low, playing tricks with the light,
Transforming fine folks into silly sights.
With burgers and lobster, a feast on the shore,
But seagulls steal bites, oh what a chore!

Echoes of the Deep

Whispers from waves make a playful sound,
As kids shout and squeal while splashing around.
"Catch me if you can!" they laugh as they flee,
But the surf is too quick, it's easy to see!

Around beach bonfires, stories are spun,
Of fish that got away, oh such fun!
With marshmallows toasted, we tell and we cheer,
Until someone burns theirs, then laughter is sheer!

Aquamarine Reveries

In splashes of color, a beach ball flies,
A seagull steals fries, oh what a surprise!
The sunburned tourists wear socks on their feet,
While crabs in their shells dance to a silly beat.

Sandcastles lean, like tipsy old men,
As waves tease the shore and retreat once again.
A flip-flop gets lost in the tide and the glee,
And the sun cream's applied like a slippery spree.

A Dance on Distant Shores

Hula hoops twirl in a merry old song,
While dolphins debate who can jump the most long.
Beach towels a-flappin' in chaos and cheer,
A sunburned chap laughs, "This is my best year!"

Shells whisper secrets in giggles and grins,
While kids battle waves with their trusty old fins.
The ice cream man yells, "A scoop for your soul!"
As sand sticks to everything, that's just the goal.

Hushed Songs of the Sea

Whispers of breezes in a sailboat so fine,
With anchors misbehaving, what a tangled line!
A sardine can chorus sings out of tune,
While crabby old fishermen grumble at noon.

An octopus juggles with seaweed galore,
"Catch me if you can!" he shouts with a roar.
The mermaids are giggling, oh what a sight,
Trading their seashells for pizza at night.

The Language of the Ocean

The ocean's got jokes that we can't quite decode,
Like barnacles plotting a great little road.
A beach chair insists it just wants to sun,
While seagulls play poker, oh, who's gonna run?

Flip-flops are chattering, each step is a treat,
As children negotiate the best sandy seat.
The tide rolls in laughter, it's all in good fun,
While crabs scribble poetry, their work never done.

Harbor of Dreams

Seagulls squawk, a real loud show,
Crispy fries, they're after, oh no!
A crab in a hat, he struts with glee,
Sipping on juice, like he's fancy as can be.

Fish flip-flop, pretending to dance,
A mermaid lost in her undersea trance.
Pirates argue over who steals lunch,
While dolphins giggle at their silly hunch.

Anchors aweigh, but where's the crew?
Off chasing seagulls, oh what a to-do!
A whale in a bow tie sings a tune,
Making the fish blush, oh what a boon!

On sandy shores, kids build a dome,
Only to watch it topple, oh how they moan.
But laughter echoes, it's clear to see,
In this harbor of chaos, we're wild and free.

Nautical Reverie

A boat with a parrot, who talks too much,
Dropping wise cracks, what a funny touch!
The captain, snoozing, lost in his dreams,
While jellyfish do a wild dance of beams.

Chests of treasures, full of old socks,
The pirate's pride? His collection of rocks.
A clam tried to sing, but it made all flee,
They laughed in the waves, 'Oh can't you see?'

Heaps of sandcastles, tall and proud,
Fallen to ruins, oh the kids cried loud!
But wait for a wave with a playful roll,
And watch as it giggles, taking its toll.

In the distance, a whale brews a potion,
While squids juggle shells with wild devotion.
The shore's a big circus, forever in play,
Where humor and tides dance the day away.

Tides That Tell Tales

Waves come crashing, a roaring cheer,
While sea stars twinkle, full of good beer.
A fisherman's tale grows taller with each sip,
He claims he caught one that was strong as a ship!

The crabs have a party, dancing on knives,
While fish in the ocean try to get lives.
A dolphin, a poet, splashes with zest,
Writing verses to put all the sea to rest.

The tide brings laughter, waves bring delight,
As mermaids giggle, showing off their light.
Over seashells and seaweed, jokes flow like gin,
In this sandy theater, where fun's never pinned.

Oh, the tide tells tales of whimsy and cheer,
As sand meets the sea, bringing all to near.
Life's too short, so grab your float,
Join the ocean's antics, and set your boat!

Seafoam Stories

Riding the tide on a noodle of foam,
A froggy old sailor claims it's his home!
With kraken and whale as his trusty mates,
Spinning wild yarns, oh how time creates!

Sea cucumbers giggle as they wriggle and slide,
While clownfish make faces, no need to hide.
A clam with a camera, snapping a shot,
Of a sea urchin that claims it's quite hot!

The waves pull in tales from far and wide,
Of fish in bow ties and porpoises' pride.
In seafoam so light, with laughter so bright,
Every splash tells a story, bringing pure delight.

From coral reefs bustling to shores of delight,
Where jellybeans swim in the glow of twilight.
This ocean of humor, so vast and so true,
Invites all to join, just bring lots of brew!

Tidepool Treasures

A crab in a hat, how very absurd,
He dances and prances, oh, what a bird!
A starfish that giggles, it rolls on the ground,
While seaweed does wiggles, all jolly and round.

The shells start to argue, who shines the best?
A clam claims a crown, while the sand's in a jest.
A fish with a mustache swims by, oh so proud,
It splashes the seafoam, creating a cloud.

A floaty sea cucumber floats with some flair,
Doing the backstroke without any care.
The tide pulls together a wacky parade,
Where laughter and chaos are merrily made.

The tidepool's a party, come join in the fun,
With critters that joke, there's never a run.
Each nook has a charm, a giggle, or two,
Where nature's a jester, all playful and new.

Dunes of Delight

The sandcastles wobbled, with turrets that lean,
While gulls stole the seashells, oh, what a scene!
A beach ball is bouncing, it rockets, then falls,
And sand in my sandwich? That's just one of the calls.

Flip-flops are fighting; they jiggle and fly,
A contest for style, oh my oh my!
The sun-baked sunscreen, now slippery slides,
We slip and we slide with our jolly old rides.

Kites dance in the breeze, like they've lost their way,
They twirl and they twist, in hilarious play.
The beachcombers giggle at footprints in line,
As starfish give pointers on how to unwind.

Oh dunes of delight, where the laughter does roam,
With sun-kissed fun seekers, we feel right at home.
No worries, just chuckles, as joy fills the space,
In the wacky warm wonder, we all find our place.

Symphony of Sea and Sky

The seagulls are soloists, squawking away,
While sand dunes provide an enthusiastic sway.
Crabs tap dance in rhythm, while shells keep the beat,
Upon this great stage where the ocean's so sweet.

The waves play the piano, a cascading sound,
Tickling our toes as we laugh on the ground.
The horizon's the conductor, waving its wand,
Creating a symphony, of seaweed and pond.

A dolphin's a soloist, leaping with glee,
It flips and it flops, like it's danced with a bee.
The fish have a chorus, so bubbly and bright,
Joining in harmony, as day turns to night.

This symphony's strange, but it hits just the right,
Notes of joy singing, from morning till night.
So come take a seat, as the show's about to start,
With giggles and splashes, it'll capture your heart.

Remnants of a Soothing Sea

Leftovers of laughter, washed up on the shore,
A flip-flop that's missing, it's looking for more.
A t-shirt that whispers, of flip-flops and fun,
With tales of the beach where the sun likes to run.

The driftwood is sculpted, a monster or two,
A fish tells its story, how funny and true.
A seashell's been practicing its graceful ballet,
While barnacles chuckle at each little display.

The sand's got some secrets, it keeps them quite sly,
Like footprints that vanish, then wink as they fly.
The tide rolls in gently, with gurgling laughs,
Taking back memories—the ocean's sweet gaffs.

Remnants of joy from a day soaked in cheer,
A world filled with giggles, a place that feels near.
So treasure those moments, let your spirit run free,
For the remnants of laughter are what's meant to be.

Serenity's Embrace in Sunlit Depths

A crab in shades sunbathes on high,
While seagulls debate how to fry.
Splashing in puddles, we giggle and dance,
As fish give us looks, like they've seen romance.

An octopus juggles in playful delight,
While dolphins form plans to take flight.
We chase all the waves with a splash and a dash,
While sand sticks to us like a glittery rash.

The Alchemy of Waves and Gold

Shells whisper secrets, they giggle, they sigh,
While sea turtles plot to take to the sky.
A flip-flop escapes, it's taking a leap,
Leaving behind a wet trail, oh so steep!

The sun's on the hunt for the best tan, you see,
Sunning itself, just like you and me.
We chase after crabs, oh what a delight,
They scurry away, just out of our sight.

Whispers of the Ocean's Caress

Salty breeze tickles our noses with glee,
As we sing off-key like a crazy bee.
The waves throw a party, they splash and they roll,
While we joyfully dive, oh, it's quite the goal!

A beach ball departs on a quest for a star,
While jellyfish float in a dance, oh so far.
We gamble with sunburn, we wager on fun,
As the sun sets our laughter's just begun!

Luminous Reflections on Sandy Shores

Funky sunglasses perched on my nose,
I strut like a peacock, everybody knows.
A sandcastle, a throne fit for quirky kings,
Where seagulls plot mischief as the laughter rings.

We ride on the waves, with splashes and squeals,
Like fish out of water, how silly it feels.
The tide comes to tickle our toes in retreat,
And we tumble and giggle, it's a comical feat!

Reflections on Dunes

On the beach, a crab does dance,
Waving claws, he takes a chance.
Laughing seagulls join the show,
While the sun steals all the glow.

A picnic spread, we munch and grin,
Sandy sandwiches, where to begin?
With chips that crunch and drinks that spill,
It's all a part of beachy thrill.

Waves come crashing, kids run by,
Building castles that touch the sky.
But when the tide starts creeping in,
Those sandy towers wear a grin.

As the day wanes, stories to share,
Of jellyfish that made us scare.
With laughter loud, we find our zone,
On this beach, we call our own.

Azure Dreams

In a floatie shaped like a duck,
I paddle far, oh what luck!
The water squeaks, it's quite a sight,
Splashing friends, a silly fight.

Umbrella shades don't shield the fun,
As sunscreen battles a burning sun.
I thought I'd tan but oh, what grief,
I'm more zebra now, slight disbelief.

Fossilized snacks and drinks on deck,
Who knew peach juice could cause a wreck?
With sticky hands, we chase the breeze,
While dodging ants and buzzing bees.

As sunset sings, our laughter glows,
With jokes about our beachside woes.
We'll roll in waves and dance like fools,
In our azure dreams, we make the rules.

Sunkissed Horizons

Sunglasses perched, I squint and smile,
Chasing shadows for a while.
The sun's a friend, it's so absurd,
It's frying brains like sunny curds.

Beach ball battles all around,
Who knew they could fly, unbound?
With every whack, someone does fall,
Then belly flops are quite the call.

Fishy tales of bites and burns,
With feisty crabs who steal our turns.
I fish for snacks, but catch a tan,
More like a lobster with no plan.

As night creeps in, the stars collide,
We roast marshmallows, giggles wide.
Sunkissed dreams and sandy songs,
Here in laughter, where all belong.

Driftwood Diaries

On driftwood logs, we plot and scheme,
To ride the waves, it's all a dream.
The tide giggles and rolls back,
While we try not to lose our snack.

Flip-flops stuck in mud so thick,
A comedic dance, a silly trick.
The waves crash high, we scream and yell,
As sand crabs watch, it's quite the sell.

A jellyfish parade, oh what fun,
We dodge and weave, we try to run.
But oops, I tripped, I'm in the blue,
Splashing down, it's nothing new.

At dusk we gather, tales are spun,
Of fish so big, almost a ton.
With laughter loud, we sign our logs,
In driftwood diaries, life's in jogs.

Tapestry of the Tides

The waves keep giggling, splash, splash,
Crabs are dancing with style, oh so brash.
Seagulls squawk jokes, they've got a knack,
While sunburnt tourists try to lay back.

Sandcastles lean, as if they drank too much,
Tip over in laughter, losing their touch.
Kids chase the foam, thinking it's a race,
While beach balls fly, like they've got no space.

Sunscreen mishaps, a slippery affair,
People slip and slide, with salty hair.
The beachside bars hum with laughter and cheer,
As someone spills juice, oh dear, oh dear!

But as the sun sets and colors merge bright,
We all share giggles, in fading daylight.
With belly laughs weaving through salty air,
We find joy wrapped in sunny good care.

Sunkissed Memories

Lounging on towels, feeling so grand,
Someone's lost their chips in the hot sand.
Footprints lead nowhere, or maybe a feast,
As dogs steal our snacks, they're the true beast!

Flip-flops are flapping, they dance the cha-cha,
While a toddler's tantrum leads to a drama.
Ice cream is melting, stickiness reigns,
It drips down our shirts while we all act insane.

Grannies are sunbathing, snoring away,
As kids build their castles, come what may.
The ice cream truck jingles, a sweet serenade,
But look out, those seagulls have come to invade!

Memories painted in shades of mishaps,
We laugh hard and loud, no time for perhaps.
With salty kisses and squishy wet feet,
The canvas of fun makes our lives feel complete.

Journeys Where the Sky Meets the Sea

We ventured to where the ocean meets sky,
Packed all our snacks, oh my, oh my!
A beach ball flops, bouncing off the rocks,
While a seagull grabs lunch, oh what a paradox!

The tide comes a'calling, splashes our toes,
Each wave is a tickle, and all good fun flows.
A kite takes flight, twisted in the wind,
While sunscreen accidents leave us all pinned.

Friends tried to surf on those boogie boards,
But ended up flopping, oh how we roared!
The pier's full of laughter, boats bobbing slow,
As the sunset paints stories that continue to glow.

So here we gather, in joyful disarray,
Finding our laughter in the games we play.
Where sky kisses sea with a humorous flair,
Creating new tales that we eagerly share.

Elegy of the Ebbing Tide

Oh, the waves roll in, then they roll out,
A game of peekaboo, without a doubt.
Boys with their buckets, trying to catch fish,
Unless they catch crabs, then it's a wish!

Old Uncle Bob thought he'd catch a wave,
But ended up crashing, a show, so brave.
His belly flopped down, a splash and a squeak,
While everyone laughed at his solo streak.

The tide pulls back, leaving shells in a line,
And conch shells whisper tales of design.
"Did you see that splash?" they say with a grin,
As a dog runs past with sand in its chin.

But as day fades and the moon takes her cue,
We chuckle at memories, both old and new.
For where fun meets folly, our laughter ignites,
In the ebbs and flows of our joyful delights.

Whispers of the Sunlit Shore

Seagulls quarrel over fries,
As sunscreen drips, oh how it flies!
Kids build castles, one foot tall,
Then watch them topple with a sprawl.

Beachballs bounce, dogs chase with glee,
Someone's caught in a jellyfish spree.
Laughter dances on the breeze,
While flip-flops float like lost keys.

Sandy toes and sunburned nose,
Sipping drinks with umbrellas like prose.
A crab sneaks by with a little strut,
While I chase my hat, oh what a rut!

Sunset glows, the day ignites,
Flip-flops crinkle in summer nights.
As laughter lingers, we lose our cares,
Telling tales of our sandy snares.

Echoes of the Turquoise Tide

The tide rolls in, a splashy play,
While seashells giggle, come what may.
Someone's snoring, sun on their face,
Crabs march on, with total grace.

Surfboards waiting, ready to ride,
Bikini tops lost, where's my pride?
Umbrellas flop in the furious breeze,
Teasing beachgoers with salty tease.

Seasick dolphins leap and twirl,
As kids squeal out in a whirl.
A lobster dance makes quite a scene,
Who knew the beach could be so mean?

As the sun dips low, we cheer and shout,
Tomorrow we'll forget the sunburned pout.
With joy and laughter, we bid goodbye,
To the day's shenanigans, oh me, oh my!

Sun-Kissed Dreams and Ocean Gleams

Burgers sizzle, grills on flame,
While sunscreen gets us into the game.
Tanned folks stumble, dance like fools,
Barefoot fun, breaking all the rules.

Ice cream drips down chins so wide,
Chasing waves with nothing to hide.
The beach ball lands on someone's head,
And laughter erupts, no one's misled.

A sandcastle proudly stands so tall,
Until Wanda's dog makes a pitiful call.
His tail knocks down what took us hours,
As we giggle amidst the beach flowers.

Evening rolls in, the stars appear,
As we toast with our drinks, no one's austere.
With sandy hugs and salty cheer,
We'll always cherish this beachy sphere.

Dunes of Glimmering Light

Sun-hats fly like kites on high,
As kids giggle and watch the seagulls fly.
Someone's lounge chair takes a trip,
And off I go with a slippery flip.

Kites tangle up in a feathered rush,
While jellybeans wilt in the sun's hush.
Beach towels spread like blankets of cheer,
Making new friends, celebrating here.

The waves crash down with a playful roar,
While someone tries to use a metal detector for more.
Finding treasures, or just beer cans,
In this arena of cozy plans.

Sunsets drape in hues of blush,
As day fades slow, we feel the rush.
Whispers of laughter mingle at night,
With glowsticks shining, oh what a sight!

Oceanic Whispers

The crabs did dance with jiggly flair,
While seagulls plotted from their lair.
A fish in shades of plaid swam by,
Said, "Nice shorts dude!" with a cheeky sigh.

The waves all chuckled, rolled in delight,
Surfboards shouting, "Hold on tight!"
We spied a dolphin with shades on sleek,
His jokes were corny, but we couldn't speak.

A turtle rolled up, quite vexed and slow,
Complaining about the beach chair row.
With every splash, the laughter swells,
As crabs recite their ocean tales.

Amid the giggles, the sun does shine,
Even the barnacles, feeling fine!
So grab a drink and let's make a toast,
To the silly sea life we love the most!

Muses of the Shore

A clam took flight, wore a tiny hat,
While sipping lemonade, just how 'bout that?
Seagulls argued 'bout who's top chef,
Flipping fish like they're the best of the best!

A starfish tried to breakdance on sand,
With three left feet, his moves were bland.
Mermaids giggled, with shells in their hair,
While fish hold auditions for the next big fair.

The sun whispered secrets to the breeze,
As the jellyfish bounced like they owned the seas.
Each wave that crashed gave rise to absurd,
With dolphins chiming in, cheerful and heard.

As laughter echoes on shores so wide,
Join the fish party, there's fun to abide.
With each splash, they sing, twist, and swirl,
Life at the beach, oh what a whirl!

Celestial Kisses of the Tide

In flip-flops, a crab strutted with pride,
Boasting his bling as the tides would glide.
Fishes texting, 'Need a date tonight?'
While seaweed tangled in a wild kite flight.

A whale serenaded with a bubble tune,
Fishy karaoke beneath the moon.
Pencils and papers made from sea grass,
Writing reviews for each beachside class.

Seashells whispered secrets, oh so deep,
While waves were dreaming of fish that leap.
The shore had tales, some silly, some grand,
Of beach volleyball played by a band.

So grab your towel, don't forget your hat,
Join the bizarre fiesta, imagine that!
A day in the sun brings giggles galore,
At this lively shore, you'll never feel sore!

The Caress of Salty Air

With every breeze, the seagulls raved,
Pointing at fishermen, all misbehaved.
A surfboard scolded its rider with flair,
"Learn to balance, don't just stand there!"

Flip-flops squeaking, a comical sound,
As folks tripped over, tumbling around.
The crab parade marched with their best moves,
Doing the conga, they jammed and grooves.

Beach balls collided like stars in the sky,
While kids threw tantrums, "Just let me try!"
A sunscreen bottle popped open with glee,
Covering everyone, even the tree!

So let's dance with the tide, feel the soft air,
As laughter erupts, taking away care.
Nature's playground, what silly delight,
Come join the fun 'til it's time for the night!

Sunlit Pathways

On a path that's shining bright,
I tripped and lost my flip-flop light.
The crabs all laughed, they joined the chase,
I ran away, a silly race.

Sunblock slathered, feeling great,
Yet missed my nose; oh, isn't fate?
Seagulls squawk, they seem to jest,
With my sandwich, they take the best.

The tide rolls in, my feet now wet,
I leap and splash, oh, what a bet!
A wave sweeps in, my hat's now gone,
I'll wear a bucket, come at dawn!

So here I stand, in laughter's glow,
With sandy toes and sunburned brow.
A day of fun, wild and carefree,
In this beachy wonder, just let it be!

Breezes Between the Palms

Winds that tickle, time for games,
I chase a kite, but oh, my shames!
It twists and twirls, then takes a dive,
   Into a drink—my straw's alive!

The palms all sway, a gentle dance,
   As I try hard to take a chance.
  With coconuts that roll around,
I'm dodging them—what have I found?

A squirrel wears my sunglasses cool,
  I laugh and think, oh, what a fool!
  He struts along, a real beach star,
   While I just sit with my bizarre.

A breeze brings whispers, salty moods,
  With laughter spilling in the foods.
  Lemonade's spilling, that's my fate,
   I'm the punchline—what a state!

Nature's Gentle Rhapsody

A turtle sneaks upon the shore,
I wave and scream, 'Hey, wait, there's more!'
But he just blinks, with slowness grand,
And leaves me waiting in the sand.

The fish all play in playful schools,
While I'm just trying to look all cool.
A splash from left, a splash from right,
I duck and dive; it's quite the sight!

Seagulls swoop, and I let go,
Of my hot dog, oh no, oh no!
They squawk and squabble, up they soar,
While I stand here yelling, "No more!"

In nature's rhythm, laughter lies,
With every wave, the humor flies.
So here I sit, bright sunlit glee,
A beachy life is meant for me!

Shores of Endless Journeys

My towel flies like a runaway kite,
I chase it down, a silly sight!
The crab waves back, gives me a cheer,
As I dive down to best my fear.

Footprints mark the sandy strand,
Though half of them seem unplanned.
I trip and tumble, face down flat,
Then splash about, "Hey, look at that!"

With seashells tossing in my bag,
A pelican comes to steal my flag.
He squawks at me, says it's his right,
I back away and start to fight!

These shores hold laughter every day,
With waves and whims leading the way.
Let's toast to fun and frisky plays,
With sandy hearts and silly ways!

Beneath Cloudless Skies

The sun is bright, a shiny coin,
We chase the kite as it does join.
A crab in sandals gets his groove,
With dance moves making all of us move.

A seagull squawks, oh what a chat,
It mocks the folks who sit and chat.
A beach ball flies, a big surprise,
And lands right in a snack bag's size.

The waves are laughing, tickling toes,
While sunscreen drips, oh how it flows!
A flip-flop flies, like a rubber bird,
The beach is wild, haven't you heard?

So come and play, wear your bright hat,
Eat sand-filled sandwiches, munch like a brat!
Under the skies, we dance and cheer,
Creating memories, year after year.

Dance of the Seabreeze

The seabreeze waltzes with our hair,
Like disco lights at an evening fair.
A dolphin dives with a silly grin,
While we just laugh, oh where to begin!

The tide rolls in like a big buffet,
We feast on shells instead of fillet.
A sandcastle crumbles, oh what a scene,
As a toddler yells, "That was my queen!"

A jellyfish floats like a balloon,
Its dance routine's set to a cartoon.
We try to boogie with our beach style,
And end up tangled, laughing all the while.

So twirl and swirl in this sunny play,
Forget the stress, just enjoy today!
The seabreeze whispers, let loose your cares,
In this funny realm, nothing compares.

Illumination at the Water's Edge

With feet in the water, we perform our tricks,
The sun's like a painter, with vibrant picks.
A clam comments, 'You dance like a fool!'
As we take a dip in the crystal pool.

The light reflects, a shimmering mess,
The beach ball rolls, oh what a stress!
A crab sneezes sand, oh what a sight,
It scuttles away, filled with fright.

The sunset giggles, turns all our snacks,
Into shadows that mimic our funny acts.
We chase after whispers, but catch just a breeze,
With laughter floating, like leaves from the trees.

So let's toast to sunsets, our toes in this muck,
As seagulls join in on our whimsical luck.
Remarkable moments, forever we'll treasure,
As laughter ignites like the sun's full measure.

Chasing the Horizon

With arms wide open, we sprint to the line,
The horizon beckons, oh isn't it fine?
A starfish plays catch with a waterlogged shoe,
And every step closer is something brand new.

The ocean giggles, splashing on shore,
While we chase jellybeans, oh so hardcore!
A dog in a floaty barks at the tide,
As we laugh at the scene, our joy can't hide.

Our footprints dance, a wiggly trace,
Each step a rhythm in this goofy race.
We laugh with the waves, race the sun's last beam,
Chasing horizons, living the dream.

So let's not forget our fun-filled spree,
These waves and chuckles, just you and me.
In a world of giggles and oceanic twists,
We'll always remember these silly bliss lists.

Embrace of the Ocean's Breath

A seagull stole my sandwich, oh what a sight,
I chased it down the beach, it took flight.
With a splash and a plop, I tripped on some sand,
Face-first in the grains, I failed to be grand.

The waves giggle softly, tickling my toes,
While I yell at the tide, 'Hey, quit with the prose!'
A crab tried to dance in a sun-faded shell,
I joined in the fun, oh, what a hard sell!

My friend, with a snorkel, looked quite the clutz,
Flipping and flopping, oh how we laugh!
He ended up tangled, quite stuck in the muck,
A fish gave him side-eye, "Hey, good luck!"

As evening falls, the beach sets the mood,
With jellyfish glowing, such a funny dude.
We gather our tales, as the sun bids goodbye,
With giggles and splashes, we just can't deny.

Palette of the Surf

My paintbrush got wet, what a terrible blunder,
Dipped in the waves, now my colors are thunder!
The tide rolls in, with a wink and a roar,
And suddenly my masterpiece's washed on the shore.

A dolphin stopped by with a curious glance,
Did it want to join in, or just learn to dance?
I handed it a brush, but it splashed the paint,
Leaving me to ponder, is this dolphin quaint?

My friend painted the sunset, but forgot the sun,
So we painted it yellow with carrots for fun!
A crow swooped down, found the scene sublime,
But snagged our snack, oh what a crime!

With laughter we roll in the soft, warm light,
Creating our chaos, oh what a delight!
Our canvas lives on, from the beach to the heart,
Mixed with the memories, it's a culinary art.

Murmurs of Distant Horizons

Tales from the shore drift along with the breeze,
A wayward crab's dance, oh, it brings me to tease.
He bowed to the waves, tripped right on his toe,
With laughter erupting, he stole quite the show.

A surfboard floats by, looking lost in the deep,
It waves at the gulls, as if calling for sleep.
A starfish chimed in, 'What's it need, a drink?'
While a passing sea turtle began to rethink.

They brewed up a storm, with shells and with foam,
Holding a party, right far from their home.
Polka-dottedfish joined, with glittering scales,
Dancing through currents, spinning their trails.

As light bids farewell, and stars begin to shine,
We join in their giggles, sipping seaweed wine.
Our hearts hold the stories, forever they stay,
In the whispers of waves, we all dance and play.

Sunrise Over the Reef

I woke up at dawn with sand in my hair,
Thought I was a mermaid, I swear, I swear!
But the waves proclaimed, 'You're more of a flop!'
As I fell in the shallows, right there with a plop.

The sun peeked out, with a grin oh so bright,
Like it knew of my tumble, it chuckled with light.
The rays tickled fish, who giggled in cheer,
While I tried to act cool, but was still in the clear.

A sea sponge came over, it was quite quite the lad,
Said, 'Join our reef party, it won't be that bad!'
But soon as I arrived, with my awkward two feet,
They all fell in line, ready for a retreat.

Yet laughter rang strong, as the day rolled ahead,
With seashells for hats, making fun of my dread.
So here's to the morning, with joy and some jest,
In the heart of the ocean, we're truly blessed.

Journey to the Edge of Daylight

Seagulls squawk, they steal my fries,
My sunburned nose, oh how it cries!
Sand between my toes, a gritty dance,
I trip over towels, miss my chance.

Umbrellas flip, they take to flight,
Chasing them down, what a sight!
Kids in the waves, splashing with glee,
While I just hope they don't drown me.

The ice cream melts, it drips and drips,
A sticky mess on my sun-kissed lips.
Beach games starting, I'm not quite quick,
I throw the ball, it's a total brick!

And as the day comes to an end,
I can't tell the sun from my tan friend.
With laughter echoed, skies fade to gray,
I guess I'll just nap til the next holiday!

Melodies of the Ocean's Light

A crab scuttles by, he looks so grand,
Holding a shell like a lifeguard's stand.
The waves shove, push, with all their might,
While I'm just here, feeling polite.

A frisbee flies, it curves through the air,
But not a soul knows just where it's fair.
Dog dives in, he's chasing a wave,
And oh, how I wish I could be brave!

My sandwich flies, a hungry bird's feast,
Though I'm still plotting for my next piece.
Sunblock smeared, looking like a ghost,
I laugh aloud, I'm a beach bum host!

As sun sets low, I dance on the shore,
Kicking up sand with each wild roar.
With tracks in the sand, I leave my roam,
Waving goodbye to my sunny home!

Whispers of the Shoreline

Shells whisper secrets, grains in a line,
I play a game that's rather benign.
Flip-flops fly off with a life of their own,
Out to the ocean, far from my throne!

In search of treasures, a cool drink in hand,
I find a giant, and it's not what I planned!
It's a beach ball stuck, what a hilarious feat,
Bouncing around, it's been quite the treat.

People in sunhats, all looking so grand,
But tripping on towels, they're losing their stand.
Sandcastle towers, they rise to the sky,
Until a rogue wave goes "I'll give this a try!"

With splashes of laughter, we all fall back,
As I wrestle my drink from a sandy attack.
With thoughts of good cheer as twilight takes sway,
I dance with the stars, end of the day!

Tides of Memory

In flip-flops I waddle, with rhythm and rhyme,
Dancing through puddles, oh, what a time!
Tiny fish wiggle, like they're in a race,
While I contemplate a sun-kissed embrace.

Towels wrapped tightly, I can't quite move,
Trying to figure out the right beach groove.
Sun hats in chaos, a colorful blend,
Every moment's laughter, never can end.

Snacks on a blanket, oh, delicious plight,
Until ants arrive, a tiny delight!
Is that a dolphin, or just Gary's hat?
I can't quite tell, but I'm loving that chat!

As the sun dips down, painting skies bright,
I dance with the waves, what a silly sight!
With memories formed, and laughter to bring,
I'll treasure this day; oh, let me take wing!

Shores of Reflection

On the beach, I lost my shoe,
But found a crab that said, "How do you do?"
It danced around, my toes in fright,
I laughed so hard, oh what a sight!

The seagulls squawked, they wanted bread,
I tossed them rolls, they flew ahead.
They squabbled over crumbs with glee,
A comical feast for you and me!

While sunbathing, I took a nap,
Woke up to find a fish in my lap.
It plopped and flopped, made quite a fuss,
"Return me now! Don't make a fuss!"

The waves were laughing, I joined their cheer,
A beachside joke, I held dear.
With seashell hats and sandy toes,
Life's a comedy, as everyone knows!

The Sea's Warm Embrace

The water's warm, yet oh so blue,
It tickles my feet, what a lovely view!
I tried a backflip, fell on my rear,
The dolphins giggled, I could hear!

A surfboard's mystery, I gave it a whirl,
Instead, I ended up in a twirl.
The lifeguard laughed, so did my friend,
"Maybe it's time to make amends!"

The beach ball bounced, it flew so high,
Beach volleyball? No chance, oh my!
It hit a sunbather, what a scene,
A playful day, the best ever seen!

As waves rolled in with a bubbly sound,
I chased my hat, it spun around.
In the end, with salt on my face,
I found pure joy in this crazy place!

Aquatic Serenades

Sing of the sea, with a splash and a boom,
A dance on the deck, with room to zoom.
The fishes joined in, with tiny sways,
A jiggling jig beneath sunray haze!

The octopus played a tune on my shoe,
While I clapped along, what else could I do?
A crab crept by, with a fancy hat,
"I'm the best dancer, imagine that!"

The gulls were crooning a melodious sound,
As I waded deeper, twirled all around.
The seaweed joined in, swaying and grinning,
In this wild concert, there's never a thinning!

The tide came in, with a whoosh and a rush,
I slipped and fell with a splash and a crush.
But laughter erupted, oh what delight,
In this watery world, everything's right!

The Light Between Waves

The sun kissed the waves, a twinkling tease,
I dove right in, hoping for ease.
A jellyfish waved, I shrieked with glee,
It's just a friend, or is it me?

The surfboards drifted with plans all awry,
"Who'll catch the next wave?" oh me, oh my!
The ocean's prankster, a slippery slide,
I rode the foam, a toppled tide!

A beach picnic, I thought I'd bring,
But sand flew in, ruining everything.
With sandwich armor and chips on my face,
I declared myself the samviest of grace!

As the sun began setting, a canvas divine,
A seagull stopped by, and stole a fried line.
With saltwater laughs, I bid the day cheer,
Tomorrow's adventure will soon be here!

Celestial Waters

Out on the beach, with ice cream in hand,
Seagulls swoop down, they're making a stand.
They want my cone, think it's their right,
But I won't give in, not without a fight!

Beach balls are bouncing, kids run about,
Splashing in waves, giving a shout.
But when I join in, I trip and I fall,
With laughter around me, I giggle and crawl.

Sunscreen applied like a thick coat of paint,
I look like a lobster, it's quite the complaint.
Everyone points, says I'm a bright hue,
But seeing me laugh, they can't help but too!

As dusk settles down, the tide starts to rise,
We roast marshmallows under twilight skies.
With sticky hands, we tell silly tales,
While the moon giggles down, as laughter prevails.

Dance of the Ocean Breeze

The wind it whistles, it pulls at my hat,
Like a mischievous cat, simply having a spat.
I chase after it, oh, what a race,
But my hat flies away, to a magical place!

Umbrellas are tumbling, chairs in a spin,
While beachgoers laugh, settling in for the win.
I think I just saw a flip-flop take flight,
Next, it'll join me in the dance of the night!

Shells scatter 'round, like confetti in glee,
As I tried to collect them, they slipped from my knee.
Digging and diving for treasures so rare,
But I just found sand, and a whole lot of hair!

The waves have their rhythm, a quirky soft beat,
Where seaweed joins in with a slithery greet.
I attempt to salsa, my partner a wave,
And I tumble right over, oh how I misbehave!

Beneath the Sunlit Canopy

Under the palms, with shade oh so nice,
I'm munching on snacks—chips crunched like ice.
A crab walks by, as if it's my mate,
I offer it chips, but it just walks straight!

Kids are building castles, each wall's a facade,
The waves come crashing, it's a sandpaper plod.
With each little wave, the castles collapse,
While giggles abound, in the sand, I am trapped!

Drinks in our hands, we toast to the sun,
But I spill mine all over—a laugh, not a fun!
It drips down my shirt, a fruity brown hue,
I guess that's a reason to sing just for you!

As the day rolls on, we sway with the breeze,
A group of odd ducks, all get on their knees.
For beach bingo, our laughter rings true,
While my friend just won—he's now covered in glue!

Picturesque Journeys

With cameras in hand, we set out to roam,
Oh, where will we go? It's a reason to comb.
Taking selfies with waves, and hats blown away,
That's a photographer's life—oh, what a display!

The sunset's a painter, with colors so bright,
But I can't find my angle, try as I might.
I end up with seagulls photobombing my shot,
Now they're the stars—it's me they forgot!

As we stroll by the shore, the sand's in my toes,
Like tiny warm hugs, as the ocean wind blows.
We pretend we're models, with poses quite grand,
But fall into giggles, as we tumble in sand.

Our journey continues, with snacks we had stashed,
Ice cream in hand, oh how quickly it splashed.
With laughter and joy, our perfect day shared,
With memories made, we go home unimpaired.

Serene Retreat of the Coastal Breeze

Flip-flops slapping, I stride with glee,
A seagull stole my fries from me.
Sunburned nose and salty hair,
I giggle at crabs that dance with flair.

Beach ball battles, oh what a sight,
Chasing it down with all my might.
Umbrellas flying, it's a circus show,
Who knew sunbathing could lead to woe?

Waves crash down with a foamy roar,
Sand in my sandwich? Just a tad more!
Towels tangled in playful knots,
Life's a beach, but where are my slots?

As the tide rolls in, I make my mark,
Building castles, oh what a lark!
Then the waves laugh, my dreams erase,
Just me and the foam, my sandy embrace.

The Color of Daydreams at Dusk

A fish in a hat, oh what a scene,
Swimming in colors where none have been.
Chasing the sunset, how fast it glows,
While my ice cream melts between my toes.

Seashells whisper in a conch shell chat,
About the gossip in the sea, imagine that!
Sandcastles tumble, it's a royal mess,
I'm king of the beach, but I must confess.

With jellyfish dances and crabby prance,
I try to join in, but lose my pants.
The tide tickles toes as it rushes so bold,
And here I am, performing, uncontrolled!

When flamingos giggle and dolphins play tag,
Life's a cartoon, with just one dragging lag.
I wave goodbye to the day's final light,
Until tomorrow, my heart takes flight.

Chasing Horizons: Where Sky Meets Sea

Kites in the air, they soar like gnomes,
I tug at the string, they take me home!
A pelican lands, looking quite grand,
I offer him snacks, we form a band.

Sandy sandwiches, what a delight,
Until a seagull takes a daring bite!
Laughter erupts as chaos unfolds,
Who needs toys when you've got beach gold?

The horizon winks, oh what a tease,
I chase it down on my knees.
A crab waves goodbye as it scuttles away,
Join me in sunset's lovely ballet!

Droplets of laughter fall from the sky,
Mixing with bubbles as we both fly.
With each twist and turn, a giggle erupts,
In chasing these dreams, I'm endlessly up.

Evocations of the Luminous Coastline

In twilight's glow, the sand starts to spark,
Fish gossip in whispers, jokes from the dark.
A dolphin outsmarting an untied shoe,
Splashing my friend as it leaps right through!

With shells as my treasures, I start to build,
But the tide has taken away all my skills.
The gulls have a laugh at my sandy plight,
I merely respond with a shrug and a bite.

Bikini-clad dreams and a kite in a swirl,
I tries to impress, but it's more like a whirl.
As the sun dips low, I fumble and grin,
In the dance of the waves, I joyfully spin.

Day fades away with a comedic sneer,
A flip-flop falters, the end is quite near.
But under the stars, we'll rhyme and we'll play,
In the magic of night, where we frolic and sway.

Lullaby of the Waves

I saw a crab with shades on tight,
He danced around, what a silly sight!
A seagull laughed, dropped a snack,
And all the fish said, 'Hey, no smack!'

Waves tickle toes, oh what a tease,
Frogs in flip flops, moving with ease.
A dolphin flipped, trying to impress,
But tripped on a wave, oh such a mess!

Turtles in line for the ice cream cone,
Claiming the flavor that was all their own.
While on the shore, a cat took a nap,
Dreaming of tuna and a sunny clap.

As the sun sets down, kids run and play,
Building castles that may wash away.
A clownfish juggles pearls in delight,
Cheering us all through the warm, funny night.

The Edge of Paradise

A parrot squawked, what's for dinner?
A fish replied with a cheeky grinner.
'We're serving seaweed, it's quite a dish!'
'Another joke? That's just delish!'

On the beach, a crab wore a tie,
He strutted about like he could fly.
His friends just snickered and rolled their eyes,
Pretending to gasp at his big surprise.

By coconut trees, a monkey swung,
Singing off-key, he wildly flung.
With every note, the waves did crash,
Echoing laughter in a splishy splash.

As the day ends, the sun bows low,
Under the palm trees, chuckles flow.
Fish with dreams of jellybean cheese,
Sway to the rhythm of the buzzing breeze.

Sunbeams on Stillness

The sun's a big pancake in the sky,
With syrupy rays, oh my, oh my!
A beach ball bounced, then rolled away,
'Catch me if you can,' it seemed to say!

Seashells gather, all trees stand tall,
Playing a game, who's the most small?
A starfish sighed, 'I'm just a star,'
The clam just laughed, 'You'll go far!'

In the distance, a whale told a joke,
Causing a splash with a playful poke.
He said, 'Why swim up when you can dive?'
The fish all giggled, feeling alive!

Under the sun, all worries flee,
With waves that whisper, 'Just let it be.'
A crab on a float, how could he lie?
Says, 'I've got my sunscreen, I'm ready to fry!'

Soft Breezes and Sweet Wishes

A soft breeze whispered through the trees,
Telling secrets to the buzzing bees.
A fish in a bowtie tried to sing,
But all that came out was a funny fling!

A hermit crab switched homes with a shoe,
Said, 'It's more fashionable, don't you think too?'
Seagulls couldn't stop their silly squawk,
As they danced around the beachside rock.

Sunflowers tried to catch a tan,
While a pufferfish dreamed of being a fan.
A seashell giggled, 'Oh what a sight!'
'Call me when it's time to party tonight!'

As the stars twinkle, they seem to say,
'Stretch out your dreams, splash in the spray!'
With laughter and joy, we find our way,
Living in moments that brighten the day.

Secrets of the Tidal Pools

Crabs in tuxedos dance with glee,
Starfish try out their yoga spree.
A clam sings operatic notes,
While seaweed takes its photoshoots.

Shy shrimp hide behind their shells,
Whispering gossip, sharing tales.
Anemones wave like they're on stage,
As seahorses strike a pose and engage.

Tiny fish throw a grand parade,
While lazy snails take their midday shade.
The tide rolls in like a sneaky thief,
Stealing the spotlight, much to our grief.

Who knew the beach had such wild trends,
With creatures making unexpected friends?
Here at the edge, where laughter flows,
Nature's sitcom—a comedy show!

Dancers of the Seafoam

Waves that crash with a playful grin,
Bubbles jump high, let the fun begin.
Jellyfish twirl in their transparent suits,
While dolphins join in, sporting their hoots.

Seagulls squawk at their feathered foes,
Convincing crabs to join in the flows.
Flip-flops flail with reckless charm,
As two suns set the dance floor warm.

Sandcastles sporting bizarre designs,
With moats of laughter where fun aligns.
The tide shimmies like a dance-off show,
And claps its sprays in a frothy glow.

Giggling shells parade on the shore,
Whispering secrets of the ocean floor.
With every wave, the jesters play,
In this aquatic ballet, on display!

The Palette of the Shore

Brushes made of seaweed stroke the day,
Painting laughter in hues of spray.
Waves slap the sand in a rhythmic beat,
While flip-flops flutter to the music's heat.

Seashells sparkle with colorful flair,
As kids make masterpieces without a care.
The tide giggles as it laps at the feet,
Stealing a splash—they retreat, then repeat.

Clouds loom like painters with a wry twist,
Brushing shadows edgily through the mist.
Crabs use their claws to artfully draw,
While the sun winks down with a playful guffaw.

What a canvas, this wide-open space,
With creatures like artists dressed for the race.
Brush up your joy, let your worries soar,
Dive into laughter upon this bright shore!

Ebb and Flow of Time

Time wobbles like jelly on the sand,
As waves chase clocks, all unplanned.
Seagulls on bicycles racing by,
Winking at fish as they defy.

Sunsets wrapped in cotton candy hues,
Tickle the tide with their silly shoes.
While the moon sneezes, stars fall to cheer,
Whispering secrets only fish hear.

The sand shifts like a playful prank,
As people tumble, having their flank.
In the ebb, we giggle, we grin,
In the flow, adventures just begin.

Time's a jester with jokes to bestow,
At this spot where the wild creatures glow.
Each moment, a treasure that dances and sways,
In a world of laughter, where joy stays!

Embracing the Horizon's Glow

A seagull steals my sandwich near,
It flaps and squawks, oh what a cheer!
Friends all laugh, I chase it fast,
But it's too late, the sandwich won't last.

The sun is shining, I'm in a race,
With sunscreen plastered all over my face.
I trip on flip-flops, a glorious fall,
Laughter erupts, I'm the star of it all.

Kids are digging, creating grand styles,
A castle that lasts only a few miles.
The tide rolls in, the castle doth weep,
I'll have to find a new plan to keep.

With ice cream dripping down to my toes,
I'm a sticky mess, but who really knows?
As laughter sparkles in the soft breeze,
We'll munch and play till we're weak in the knees.

Sun-Drenched Shores of Bliss

Sandy toes wriggle, a cat in the sun,
The way it sprawls, it thinks it's so fun.
But watch it leap, oh what a sight,
Lands in my drink, now that's pure fright!

Umbrella drinks with tiny little straws,
We sip and giggle, applause and guffaws.
A friend drops their hat, it flies like a kite,
Chasing it down is a comical sight.

Beach balls are bouncing, the games are intense,
I serve a volley, but land on the fence.
The ball flies back with a cheeky laugh,
And I'm thinking, "Why did I choose this path?"

Sunsets are gleaming, we wave goodnight,
Tomorrow we'll play with the same sheer delight.
With laughter echoing, we shall return,
For more silly moments, we'll gladly yearn.

The Dance of Light on Gentle Waves

The surfboard wobbles, I stand on the edge,
As I tumble over, I make a new pledge.
To conquer the waves, like a true champ,
But splash like a fish? It's just a small stamp.

Fins and flippers, oh what a sight,
A crab scuttles past, what a goofy fright.
It pinches my toe, I yell out in glee,
While my friends are rolling, laughing at me.

Shells and seaweed all stuck in my hair,
As I hop on the sand, I dance without care.
A seagull joins in, I stamp my two feet,
A silly dance-off, isn't life sweet?

Each wave that crashes brings joy anew,
In this sandy playground, all feellike a crew.
We'll ride every giggle, every great twirl,
Painting the day with fun, oh what a whirl!

Reflections of a Brilliant Sun

With sunglasses on, strutting down the shore,
I trip on nothing; oh, I need a little more.
I wave to the folks, who chuckle and grin,
'This sunset's great but look at my chin!'

The sand's a furnace, my feet dance and scream,
But ice cream beckons, fulfilling my dream.
I drop a scoop, it lands like a blob,
But who really cares? It's all just a mob!

Beach towels spread, we gather to feast,
Hot dogs and chips, an absolute beast.
But the seagulls swoop down, eyeing our tray,
In seconds, they vanish, oh what a ballet!

The mirror-like sea reflects our delight,
As we snack and share stories till the night.
With laughter and joy, the memories weave,
Let's embrace the silly; more fun we'll achieve!

Azure Embrace of the Sea

On a day so bright, with a big beach ball,
I tried to impress, but I tripped and did fall.
I splashed like a fish, my dignity lost,
My friends just laughed; oh, what a cost!

Seagulls were circling, with eyes full of greed,
My sandwich in hand, they plotted their deed.
One swooped in fast, it stole my lunch stash,
I waved my fists, made a comical splash!

The waves came and tickled my toes with a grin,
I bounced like a puppy, ready to win.
But slippery rocks turned my joy into plight,
Slid down with a giggle, what a silly sight!

Sunset came down, with colors so bright,
I dressed like a crab; oh, what a delight!
With shells for my shoes, I danced on the shore,
Who knew such mishaps could lead to such more!

Radiant Horizons and Lapping Waves

The tide was so low, we thought we could walk,
But quicksand got us, oh, what a shock!
Grains in my shoes, and sand in my hair,
I giggled and squealed, 'It's the beach's fair share!'

Catch me a crab, I said with a grin,
But it pinched my finger, I nearly fell in.
My friends laughed so hard, with drinks in their hands,
Who knew crustaceans had such funny plans?

A torch broke the dusk, we made shadows that danced,
I twisted and turned, not a moment to chance.
The ocean looked on, with a wave and a sigh,
As my friends cheered me on, I gave it a try!

Back to our towels, we plopped with a thud,
With sand in our snacks, we laughed till we were mud.
So here's to the fun, and the giggles we crave,
At the edge of the world, where we act like we brave!

Tides of Warmth and Liquid Sky

The sun dressed us up in a warm, golden hue,
Yet somehow my sunscreen just missed quite a few.
I turned into crimson, a lobster on deck,
My friends just snickered, what a goofy wreck!

We raced for the waves, like kids on a spree,
But we dove too soon—right into the sea!
Flipped like a seal, I floundered so free,
With foam in my hair, a slick sight to see!

The thought of a tan was quickly displaced,
As ice cream cones started to run down my waist.
One sip of my drink turned into a fight,
When a seagull swooped down, oh, what a sight!

As twilight approached, we sat on the sand,
Sharing our stories, both silly and grand.
With laughter abound 'neath the starry ignite,
We toasted the fun—what a jovial night!

Sunlit Tranquility by the Coast

In a beach chair I lounged, oh, what a show,
With my hat so wide, it stole the view, you know!
I turned just in time, and the wind gave a shush,
Sandy chips flew, oh what a scrumptious rush!

My friend tried to surf, with style and grace,
But the board did a dance; he lost the race!
With splashes so mighty, he flopped with a splash,
I laughed till I cried; oh, what a clash!

We buried my pal, right up to his neck,
With shells all around, and a big sunblock speck.
He shouted and squirmed, and it caught on the breeze,
Started a laughter, that nobody could freeze!

As the horizon blushed with the dusk of the day,
We sang silly songs in a gleeful array.
With smiles on our faces and joy in our hearts,
This beach will forever hold our goofy parts!

The Color of Peace

A beachball rolls, it flies in the air,
Landing on Larry, without a care.
Sunburned noses, laughter all around,
We're kings of the castle, can't be knocked down.

Sandcastles crumble, but not our glee,
A seagull swoops by, stealing our brie.
With each little wave, we giggle and shout,
Who knew the sea could bring such a route?

Flip-flops stuck, we stumble and laugh,
Chasing our dreams on a sailboat's half.
The tide's pulling out, our snacks drift away,
Every mishap turns into a play.

Belly flops echo through each gleeful splash,
While jellyfish dance, we run and dash.
Here on this stretch, it's all pure delight,
We'll dance with the waves until the night.

Horizons Unfurled

The horizon giggles, it makes such a tease,
While we try to catch it, it sways in the breeze.
Kites soaring high, they have minds of their own,
We're tangled in strings, but never alone.

A crab in a top hat looks quite debonair,
He scuttles away, we follow with care.
But as we rush forth, we trip on our shoelaces,
The dance of the day, with giggles and paces.

Drifting on floats, like ducks in a row,
Splashing up water, we all steal the show.
Our picnic's a mess; oh, where is the cake?
But look at the fun that we're dying to make!

As twilight approaches, we gather our tales,
Of funny misfortunes and stubbornails.
Castaways of joy, we wave to the sun,
With lightness afoot, like it's all just begun.

Glistening Dreams

In the surf, we squabble, over shells cracked and neat,
Who's got the best one? With sand on our feet.
A treasure awaits from the bubbling foam,
We dig like real pirates, we feel right at home.

Sunhats become sails, as winds start to blow,
We tip like tightrope walkers, oh no, oh no!
With waves rolling in, our antics take flight,
As seagulls take bets on our flip of delight.

Sunscreen fiascoes, all in the air,
"Did I miss a spot?!" we laugh without care.
But look at the sparkle, the laughter we bring,
Dreams glisten bright, it's a magical fling.

As stars peek above, like diamonds on show,
With sand in our hair, we put on a glow.
Night's final act, with giggles to share,
We drift into dreams, of fun everywhere.

Footsteps on the Coast

A trail of footprints, lost in the sand,
Who stepped on who? It's all quite unplanned.
As shuffle and slide, we chase the retreat,
Each wave steals our giggles, we can't be beat.

Oh look! The sandmen have come out to play,
With bucket and spade, they refuse to stray.
Eyelashes dripping with seawater surprise,
They point at the crab who is rolling his eyes.

We bask in the sun, like lizards at rest,
Chasing our shadows, this day is the best.
Each splash brings a story, each dip brings a cheer,
Funny little moments, the laughter we hear.

As darkness approaches, we gaze 'cross the spray,
With hands linked together, we dance the night away.
On this beach of wonders, how time flies so fast,
Yet the joy that we've shared? It forever will last.

www.ingramcontent.com/pod-product-compliance
Lightning Source LLC
Chambersburg PA
CBHW072219070526
44585CB00015B/1412